LifeWay Kids & FOR GIRLS L. PRESENT

God's Brave Girl

A COURAGEOUS JOURNEY OF FAITH

YOUNGER GIRLS STUDY JOURNAL
LIFEWAY PRESS®
NASHVILLE, TN

Requests for permission should be addressed in writing to LifeWay Press®
One LifeWay Plaza
Nashville, TN 37234-0172

ISBN 978-1-535999-11-3
Item 005823180

Dewey Decimal Classification Number: 268.432
Subject Heading: Discipleship—Curricula\God\Bible—Study
Dewey Decimal Classification Number: 248.82
Subject Heading: CHRISTIAN LIFE \ JESUS CHRIST—TEACHINGS

Printed in the United States of America
LifeWay Kids
LifeWay Resources
One LifeWay Plaza
Nashville, Tennessee 37234-0172

Cover design: Julia Ryan

We believe the Bible has God for its author; salvation for its end; and truth, without any mixture of error, for its matter and that all Scripture is totally true and trustworthy. To review LifeWay's doctrinal guideline, please visit lifeway.com/doctrinalguideline.

All Scripture quotations are taken from the Christian Standard Bible®, Copyright 2017 by Holman Bible Publishers. Used by permission. Christian Standard Bible® and CSB® are federally registered trademarks of Holman Bible Publishers.

About the Authors

Jonathan & Wynter Pitts:
FOUNDERS OF FOR GIRLS LIKE YOU

Wynter Pitts is the author of several books and the founder of For Girls Like You, a bimonthly magazine that equips girls to be who God has created them to be and to resource their parents to raise strong, Christ-following girls. Wynter tragically passed from death to life on July 24, 2018, after 15 years of marriage to her beloved Jonathan.

Jonathan Pitts is an author, speaker, and executive pastor at Church of the City in Franklin, Tennessee, where he lives with his four daughters. Prior to pastoring, Jonathan was executive director at The Urban Alternative, the national ministry of Dr. Tony Evans in Dallas, Texas.

Danielle Bell:
A GIRL JUST LIKE YOU!

Danielle has over 24 years of children's ministry experience and is a respected children's ministry leader and trainer. She has spoken regionally and nationally at children's ministry conferences (i.e., *Children's Pastors Conference, ETCH, KidMin conference*). She has written for *The Gospel Project for Kids*, and she currently works with *Outreach Media Group* writing preschool and elementary lessons for *Sermons4Kids*. She also teaches as part of the children's ministry certification program at beadisciple.com. Danielle's blog, dandibell.com, was named one of the top 100 kids ministry blogs by ministry-to-children.com.

Table of Contents

A Note from the Pitts Sisters
ALENA, KAITLYN, CAMRYN, & OLIVIA

HI THERE!

We are the Pitts sisters—Camryn, Olivia, Kaitlyn, and Alena—girls just like you! We are so excited you are holding this journal made just for you! Our mom and dad started an awesome ministry called *For Girls Like You* because they wanted girls just like you and us to know more about God. This journal is going to teach you all kinds of cool stuff about God, how much He loves you, and the courageous journey of faith He has planned for you.

We've learned a lot about bravery over the last few years. You see, two years ago our mommy went to heaven to be with Jesus. We've missed our mom so much since she's been gone, but we believe God is still with us. He sees us. He knows us, and He loves us.

And we believe the same thing is true for you. God loves you so much, and He wants you to learn more about what it means to live as His brave girl in the world around you. The more you know Him, the more you learn about yourself!

Our mom wanted us, and girls like us, to learn about God so that we can walk passionately and boldly in who God has created us to be. We hope this journal helps you as you learn more about God and more about yourself! Remember, God made you, and He loves you! He calls you to live fearlessly and to bravely follow Him and His big plans for your life!

Camryn, Olivia, Kaitlyn, and Alena

How Do I Use This Study Journal?

This Study Journal is designed just for you! On the first few pages of each session you will find the Bible story you will learn about and fun activities to do with other girls in your group.

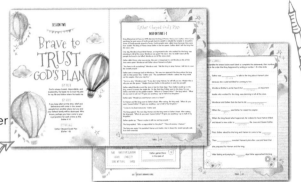

Then, there are pages set apart for you to use on your own each week. These pages will help you spend time with God, pray, and learn more about yourself.

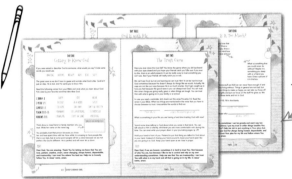

Finally, don't forget about the extra fun stuff! Be on the lookout for extra fun games, riddles, puzzles, and more! We hope you love your journal and use it as you learn more about God, His good plans for your life, and how to bravely live for Him on this courageous journey of faith!

Brave to BELIEVE GOD

KEY TRUTH

Jesus came to make my relationship with God possible. He calls me to believe He is who He says He is.

KEY VERSE

I have come so that they may have life and have it in abundance.
John 10:10 (CSB)

KEY PASSAGE

Mary Saw Jesus
(John 20:1-18)

Mary Saw Jesus
BASED ON JOHN 20:1-18

On the third day after Jesus' death, Mary Magdalene (MAG duh leen) went out to Jesus' tomb. It was still dark, and she saw that the large stone at the entrance had been moved away.

Mary ran to Simon Peter and John. "They have taken the Lord out of the tomb, and we don't know where they have put Him!" she said.

Peter and John ran to the tomb. John looked inside and saw the linen cloths lying there. Then Peter went into the tomb and saw the linen cloths, too. The cloth that had been around Jesus' head was folded up. John believed that Jesus was alive. Then Peter and John went back home.

Mary stood outside the tomb and cried. When she looked inside, she saw two angels sitting there. They said to her, "Woman, why are you crying?"

"Because they've taken away my Lord, and I don't know where they've put Him," she said. Then Mary turned around. Jesus stood in front of her, but she did not recognize Him.

Jesus said, "Woman, why are you crying? Who are you looking for?"

Mary thought Jesus might be the gardener. She replied, "Sir, if you have taken Jesus away, tell me where you've put Him and I will go get Him."

Jesus said, "Mary."

Mary turned around and said, "Teacher!" Jesus sent Mary to tell the other disciples that He was going back to the Father. Mary did what Jesus said and told the disciples, "I have seen the Lord!"

I HAVE SEEN THE LORD

Listen and follow along as these Bible verses are read aloud. Use your imagination to think about what expression may have been on Mary's face at different parts of the story. As your listen, draw what you think Mary Magdalene's face may have looked like during each part of this true story.

1 JOHN 20:1-2
2 JOHN 20:3-11
3 JOHN 20:12-13
4 JOHN 20:14-15
5 JOHN 20:16-18

KEY CODE

Solve the code using the key to reveal today's key truth.

Jesus Came To Make My
ReLaTioNship WiTH GoD
PoSSiBLe. He CaLLS me To
BeLieVe He iS WHo He
SayS He iS.

B 👑   M ⭐
C ☀   N 〰
D 🖤   P ❄
G 🌼   R 🖤
H ☆   S ⚓
J 🌻   T 🖤
K ✕   V ☆
L 🌸   W 👑

JESUS IS WORTH SEEING

Look up each passage in a Bible and fill in the blanks to help describe who Jesus is. Draw a star by the Bible passage that means the most to you.

01. **JOHN 6:35 (CSB)**

    "I am the bread of _life_ ," Jesus told them. "No one who comes to me will ever be hungry, and no one who believes in me will ever be thirsty again."

02. **JOHN 8:12 (CSB)**

    Jesus spoke to them again: "I am the light of the _world_ . Anyone who follows me will never walk in darkness, but will have the _light_ of life."

03. **JOHN 10:7 (CSB)**

    Jesus said again, "Truly I tell you, I am the _gate_ for the _sheep_ ."

04. **JOHN 10:11 (CSB)**

    "I am the good _Shepherd_ . The _good_ shepherd lays down his life for the sheep."

05. **JOHN 11:25 (CSB)**

    Jesus said to her, "I am the resurrection and the _life_ . The one who believes in me, even if he dies, will live."

06. **JOHN 14:6 (CSB)**

    Jesus told him, "I am the _way_ , the truth , and the _life_ . No one comes to the Father except through me."

07. **JOHN 15:5 (CSB)**

    "I am the _vine_ ; you are the branches. The one who remains in me and I in him produces much fruit, because you can do nothing without _me_ ."

DAY ONE
God Is Everywhere

Nope, it can't happen. There is no place you can be that God isn't there with you. He is everywhere. Now, while that may sound confusing to us, that is just a part of who God is. God is omnipresent *(om KNEE press ant)*. That's a big, fancy word that means God is everywhere all the time. When Mary was crying at Jesus' tomb, He was there. That time you were hurt by a friend, He was there. The last time tears rolled down your face, He was there, too. He is with you right now as you read these words. Pretty amazing, right?

Once we understand that God is everywhere, we realize that the key to living in bravery is believing He is with us even when we do not see Him. That's having faith. Faith means believing and trusting in something you do not see. Let's check that out in the Bible:

Open your Bible to Hebrews 11:1. Fill in the missing words to the Bible verse on the lines provided below.

NOW ___faith___ IS THE ___confidence___ OF WHAT IS ___hoped___ FOR,

THE ___assurance___ OF WHAT IS NOT ___seen___. (CSB)

It's not our job to be everywhere, but God calls us to believe He is everywhere, even when we can't see Him. When is a time you need to be reminded that God is with you?

Next time you are there and you need to be brave, remind yourself that God is right there with you. You can trust Him and believe that He is always with you!

PRAY

Dear God, sometimes it can be hard for me to believe You are with me when I can't see You. I need to know You are always with me so that I can be brave to trust You. You are everywhere. Will You help me remember that the next time I am afraid or feel alone? In Jesus' name, amen.

DAY TWO
The Bible Is True and Is for You

What is your favorite book? Maybe it is a mystery book, a book about someone you admire, or a fun series about friends. I bet those are all fun books to read, but do you think those books can change your life? They may help you think new thoughts, learn things, or make small changes, but there is only one book that can change your life forever. Can you guess what it is? (Hint: The answer is in the title. Circle it!)

We often think of the Bible as a book with lots of different stories, but it is actually one book with lots of parts that tell one big story. And guess what? It's a story about God's love for you! How can you know? Let's look at one of the most popular verses in the Bible—John 3:16. As you read the verse below, put a 🖤 over the part that talks about love. Put a ✝ where it talks about God's Son Jesus. Finally, put a 🙂 near the great news of this verse.

FOR GOD LOVED THE WORLD IN THIS WAY: HE GAVE HIS ONE AND ONLY SON, SO THAT EVERYONE WHO BELIEVES IN HIM WILL NOT PERISH BUT HAVE ETERNAL LIFE.
JOHN 3:16 (CSB)

Did you know that Jesus came to change your life forever? He did! Jesus came so that you could be brave to believe God and have a relationship with Him. Because we think, say, and do things that go against God's best for us, our relationship with God is broken. It's kind of like when you say something unkind to a friend. That friendship is broken until you apologize and your friend forgives you. In a similar way, we need help fixing our broken relationship with God, and that's why Jesus came.

God's Word, the Bible, tells us in John 3:16 (and in many other verses) that God loves us. Just think of how your life would change if you opened the Bible and read what God had to say to you!

PRAY

Dear God, thank You for the Bible. Will You help me want to read the Bible more to learn what You want to tell me? Through the Bible, help me understand that Jesus came so that I could have a relationship with You. In Jesus' name, amen.

I Am Adopted

Being adopted means you are part of a new family. Maybe you have been adopted into a new family or your family has adopted a child or even a new pet.

Adoption is pretty amazing! Did you know that if we have a relationship of faith with God, we are adopted? How do we have a relationship with God? Well, Jesus came to make our relationship with God possible.

Open your Bible to Ephesians 1:5. Read the verse aloud three times. Then without looking at the verse, answer this question:

Who does God adopt us through? (Circle your answer.)

A HOSPITAL   JESUS CHRIST   THE BIBLE

That's right! When we realize we are sinners in need of a Savior, we are adopted into God's family through Jesus. Jesus is the only way to God. He came to earth to pay the price for our sins by dying on the cross. But Jesus didn't stay dead— He defeated death.

Remember in our story this week that Mary was brave to believe that Jesus was alive even after she had seen Him crucified. How do we know Mary was brave to believe God? Unscramble what she said to the disciples.

I _____ _____ ____ ____. JOHN 20:18 (CSB)
    veha   ense   hte   drLo

PRAY

Dear God, thank You for sending Jesus so I could be adopted into Your family. Help me understand that Jesus came to fix my broken relationship with You. Thank you for sending Jesus for me. Help me be brave to believe You are who You say You are. In Jesus' name, amen.

Truth

Mark true or false for the following statements.

(T) (F) There is more than one God.

(T) (F) Jesus only loves me when I am good.

(T) (F) The world created itself.

All of the aboves answers are false. How do we know? Because God's Word says so. Sometimes we believe things because someone tells us or something just sounds good, but we have a source for truth—God's Word.

Did you know that when the government trains people to find fake money, they don't take time to study all the crazy, fake money people make? They spend hours studying the real money so they know when they find a fake.

This is how it should be for us and God's Word. We should spend lots of time in it so that we know when someone says something that is not true in God's Word.

Open your Bible to 2 Timothy 3:16-17.

Circle the things below that this verse says the Bible is good for:

TEACHING   COLORING   REBUKING   TRAINING

SLEEPING   CORRECTING   COOKING   PLAYING

If we want to live as God's brave girls and believe God, we need to spend time in His Word to know what it says. God wants you to know His truth so you can be brave to believe He is who He says He is.

PRAY

Dear God, thank You for the truth of Your Word. Show me things in my life that may be wrong when compared to Your Word. Help me know Your Word and make it the source for what I believe. Help me believe so I can be brave and share Your truth with others. In Jesus' name, amen.

DAY FIVE
God Never Changes

Change cannot be stopped. The weather changes, your friends change, even the things you like will change. In the circle provided, draw how you feel about change.

There is good news. When everything around you is changing, God stays the same.

Read Malachi 3:6 below. Underline the part that proves to you that God does not change.

> "BECAUSE I, THE LORD, HAVE NOT CHANGED, YOU DESCENDANTS OF JACOB HAVE NOT BEEN DESTROYED." MALACHI 3:6 (CSB)

If we are going to be brave, we don't look at our circumstances or world for confidence because they are always changing. Our source of confidence is God. He never changes, and in Him alone we can live brave lives. With your pen, color in the promise in the picture below.

PRAY

Dear God, it is great news to hear that You do not change. When the world is changing around me, remind me to look to You, knowing I can depend on You to never change. You are who You say You are. In Jesus' name, amen.

Change will keep coming. God never changes.

Journaling

Is there anything God is teaching you about Himself this week?
Have you learned anything about yourself?
Is there anything you want to spend time talking to God about?

Use these journal pages to write out your thoughts, questions, and prayers to God. Thank Him for teaching you about how to live as His brave girl, trusting in Him no matter what!

Things to Talk to God About

_____   _____

_____   _____

_____   _____

_____   _____

_____   _____

_____   _____

Games & Such

```
G X B V S I A J F S T W
E B R A V E O V R N R M
Z E Q I H K T Q A T U D
O L P N S F M D X K T I
B I O V A E N A C D H S
A E P O D U N D J U A C
E V L M B H K C E N L I
R E L A T I O N S H I P
P D I L T M G T U C V L
N Q F K R A J Y S I E E
R G E S T R O N G U B Q
A P Q O X Y H C P J N O
```

Find the following words in the word search:
BRAVE STRONG JESUS ALIVE
DISCIPLE RELATIONSHIP MARY BELIEVE

How many words can you make out of:
RELATIONSHIP

_____   _____

_____   _____

_____   _____

_____   _____

Who are some brave girls you know? Why are they brave?

_____

_____

_____

Brave to TRUST GOD'S PLAN

KEY TRUTH

God is always honest, dependable, and trustworthy. He wants me to trust His plan for my life and follow where He leads me.

KEY VERSE

If you keep silent at this time, relief and deliverance will come to the Jewish people from another place, but you and your father's family will be destroyed. Who knows, perhaps you have come to your royal position for such a time as this.
Esther 4:14 (CSB)

KEY PASSAGE

Esther Obeyed God's Plan
(Esther 1–8)

Esther Obeyed God's Plan
BASED ON ESTHER 1-8

King Ahasuerus (uh haz yoo EHR uhs) was the king of Persia. Many years earlier, when Cyrus was king, he sent some of God's people back to Judah to rebuild the temple in Jerusalem. Some of God's people stayed in Persia. God's people were called Jews because they were from Judah. The king of Persia chose Esther to be his queen. Esther didn't tell the king that she was a Jew.

One day, Mordecai (MOR de ki) (Esther's cousin) heard that Haman, an important leader who worked for the king, was planning to kill all the Jews. Mordecai was upset! He was a Jew; he didn't want all the people he loved to be killed. Mordecai and all the Jews cried.

Esther didn't know what was wrong. She sent a messenger to ask Mordecai why all the Jews were upset. Mordecai told Esther about Haman's evil plan.

"You have to do something!" Mordecai said. "Ask the king to stop Haman. Ask him to save the Jewish people."

Esther sent a message back to Mordecai. "No one can approach the king unless the king calls for that person first," Esther said. "The punishment is death—unless the king holds out his scepter; then you may live."

"You're a Jew," Mordecai said. "If you don't stop Haman, he will kill you, too. Maybe this is why you are the queen." Maybe God put Esther in the palace to save her people!

Esther asked Mordecai and the Jews to fast for three days. Then Esther would go to the king, even if it meant she might die. On the third day, Esther went to the king. He saw Esther and held out his golden scepter. "What is it, Queen Esther?" the king asked. "What do you want to ask me? I'll give you anything—up to half of my kingdom."

Esther said, "Would you and Haman come to a feast?"

So Haman and the king went to Esther's feast. After eating, the king said, "What do you want, Queen Esther? I'll give you anything—up to half of my kingdom."

"Come to my feast tomorrow," Esther said.

The king agreed. The next day, Haman and the king went to Esther's feast. After eating, the king said, "What do you want, Queen Esther? I'll give you anything—up to half of my kingdom."

Esther spoke up, "There is a plan to kill me and my people." The king replied, "Who is responsible for this plan?" "This evil enemy—Haman!" Esther said.

The king was angry! He punished Haman and made a law to keep the Jewish people safe from their enemies.

ALL ABOUT ESTHER

Each of the verses listed reveals something we know about Esther and her trust in God. Connect each verse to its matching phrase. Then fill in the blanks by looking up the reference in your Bible for the answers. Use the word bank for help!

ESTHER 2:7

ESTHER 5:2

ESTHER 2:10

ESTHER 2:15

ESTHER 4:4

ESTHER 2:7

ESTHER 7:3

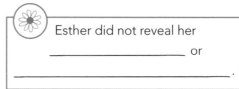
Esther did not reveal her
_____ or
_____.

Esther was
_____.

As soon as the king saw Esther standing in the courtyard, she gained _____ with him.

Esther had no
_____
or _____ .

The queen was overcome with _____ .

Esther said, "If I have found favor with you, Your Majesty, and if the king is pleased, spare my life; this is my request. And
_____;
this is my desire."

Esther gained favor in the eyes of
_____.

WORD BANK:

MOTHER   BEAUTIFUL
EVERYONE WHO SAW HER
FEAR   FAMILY BACKGROUND
FATHER   ETHNICITY
SPARE MY PEOPLE   FAVOR

STORY SCRAMBLE

Unscramble the letters below each blank to complete the statements, then number them in the order that they happened by writing a number 1-8 in the circle.

○ Esther was _____ to talk to the king about Haman's plan
driafa
because she could be killed for coming to him.

○ Mordecai (Esther's cousin) heard that _____, an important
mHaan
leader who worked for the king, was planning to kill all the Jews.

○ Mordecai told Esther that she had to do _____.
mhostieng

○ When the _____ saw Esther, he extended his scepter.
gkni

○ When the king heard what happened, he ordered to have Haman killed
and issued a new order to _____ the Jews and Queen Esther.
cptrote

○ First, Esther asked for the king and Haman to come to her _____.
tseaf

○ Then _____ revealed Haman's plot after a second feast that
etshEr
she prepared for Haman and the king.

○ After fasting and praying for _____ days, Esther approached the king.
eehtr

DAY ONE
Getting to Know God

If you were asked to describe God to someone, what would you say? Circle some words you would use.

AMAZING   BORING   MIGHTY   HOLY   REAL   SILLY

The great news is, we don't have to guess and wonder what God is like. God isn't just an idea; He is real, and He wants you to know Him.

Read the following verses from your Bible and circle what you learn about God. Put a star by your favorite word that describes God.

1 JOHN 4:8	HAPPY	LOVE	MEAN
2 PETER 3:9	PATIENT	IN A HURRY	SASSY
GENESIS 1:1	CREATOR	FAR AWAY	CAN'T BE TRUSTED
PSALM 33:13-15	UNAWARE	SEES EVERYTHING	IS SURPRISED
HEBREWS 13:8	CHANGING	STAYS THE SAME	UNLOVING

HELLO MY NAME IS:

Think about a close friend or family member who you trust. Write her name on the name tag.

You probably trust that person because you know her and have spent time with her. It is amazing to have people like that in our lives, but at some point people will let us down because we are not perfect. But God is different. He is perfect and will never let us down.

PRAY

Dear God, You are amazing. Thank You for letting me know that You are loving, patient, creative, smart, never changing, always honest, dependable, and trustworthy. I can trust You where You lead me. Help me to bravely follow You. In Jesus' name, amen.

DAY TWO

The Trust Game

Have you ever done the trust fall? You know, the game where you fall backward with your eyes closed and you hope your friends catch you? (Be sure if you ever try this, there is an adult present.) It can be really scary to trust something you can't see, like if your friends will really catch you or not.

We can't see God, but we are learning we can trust Him! It can be hard to trust God sometimes because He doesn't always do things like we would. Actually, His ways are not like our ways because He is so much smarter. Don't get caught up in how you feel, because the good news is, you can always trust God. You can trust Him when things are going really great or when things are tough. You can trust Him with what is going on in your family or at school.

In case you need a reminder, let's check out Proverbs 3:5. Read the verse in your Bible. What two things are mentioned in the verse that you have to choose between to trust? Unscramble the words to find out.

_____   _____
       hte dLro   uryo duneinrgsandt

What is something in your life you are having a hard time trusting God with now?

_____

Spend some time talking to God about what you wrote in that blank. You can talk aloud to Him or silently, whichever you are more comfortable with during this time. You can even write your prayer down in your journaling pages (p. 27).

Hold out your hand in front of you. Pretend to put that thing you talked to God about in your hand. Instead of closing your hand around it, leave your hand open like you are giving it to God. Keep your hand open as we close in prayer.

PRAY

Dear God, if we are honest, sometimes it is hard to trust You. Not because of who You are, but because we like to be in control and rely on our own understanding sometimes. Help me see that You are trustworthy. I can trust You with what is in my hand and all that is going on in my life. In Jesus' name, amen.

DAY THREE
God Is with Me

Have you ever had something break your heart? It really hurts, doesn't it? Maybe someone you loved has passed away or is sick. Maybe someone broke a promise to you. In the broken heart picture, write or draw something that has made you sad.

Do you ever wonder where God is when bad things happen? If you do, then today's Bible verse will be very helpful to you.

Read Psalm 34:18. Where does it say God is to people who are brokenhearted?

_____

erna

When your heart is breaking, you can trust that God is near. Remember, we learned that He is kind, He never changes, He is dependable, and He is trustworthy.

What do you have in your life that He can't handle? (Circle the correct answer.)

NOTHING   A COUPLE OF THINGS   EVERYTHING

PRAY

Dear God, thank You for being so close to me when my heart hurts. Help me see You right in the middle of hard times. Help me know that even when life hurts really badly, I can trust Your plan. In Jesus' name, amen.

Is It Too Much?

What is something that you love that you collect or have lots of? Draw a picture of that item. After you draw a picture, try to count in your mind how many of those items you have and put that number in the circle.

#

What is something that you could never do without? Maybe it is something you sleep with or a friend you have. Draw a picture of it in the box.

We love stuff, don't we? Some stuff we think we can never have enough of, and some stuff we can't imagine living without. Things in general are not bad, but when we look to those things to make us happy, we can take our focus off of God, who gives us good gifts, and put our focus on the stuff He gives us. We can also place our trust in those items and not in God.

Open your Bible to Psalm 9:10. Fill in the blanks.

Those who know His name _____.

usrtt ni mHi

God does not abandon those who _____.

ekes imH

PRAY

Dear God, if I am honest, sometimes I can be greedy and want way too much of something. Sometimes I put my trust in other things besides You. Will You help me trust You? Help me not to put anything in Your place but to seek You first. Thank You, God, for always being honest, dependable, and trustworthy. Help me trust Your plan for my life and follow where You lead me. In Jesus' name, amen.

DAY FIVE
Who He Is

How would you feel if you got a new device and your friend only wanted to come over to play with it? What if she ignored you and just played with your stuff? Then when it wasn't new anymore, what if she didn't want to spend time with you?

You know, sometimes we do this with God. We know how great He is and how He is there for us, but we can love the stuff God does for us more than we love Him.

Think about the last few times you talked to God. Write what you talked to Him about on the blanks below.

_____   _____   _____

Were you mostly asking Him for something, or were you enjoying spending time talking to Him? (Circle your answer.)

ASKING HIM FOR STUFF   ENJOYING HIM FOR WHO HE IS

God is our Heavenly Father. He loves to give us good gifts, but He doesn't want us to love Him for the stuff He gives us. Here is a tough question. If God didn't give you anything else for the rest of your life, would you still love Him?

YES   NO

What does God tell us in John 14:15 we will do if we love Him?

_____

We don't keep God's commands to prove our love to Him. God's love is given to us freely. It isn't something we have to earn. Because we love God, our hearts are motivated to love Him more and follow what He tells us to do.

PRAY

Dear God, we love You. Help me love You more and more each day. Help me love You for who You are, and because of my love for You, help me to obey Your commands. In Jesus' name, amen.

Journaling

Is there anything God is teaching you about Himself this week?
Have you learned anything about yourself?
Is there anything you want to spend time talking to God about?

Use these journal pages to write out your thoughts, questions, and prayers to God. Thank Him for teaching you about how to live as His brave girl, trusting in Him no matter what!

Things to Talk to God About

_____   _____

_____   _____

_____   _____

_____   _____

_____   _____

_____   _____

Games & Such

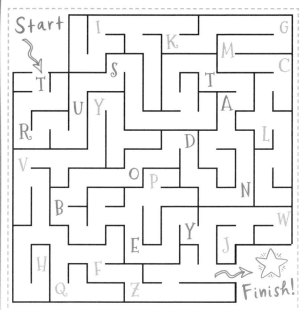

Start

I K M G
T S C
U Y T A
R D L
V O P N
B W
E Y J
H F
Q Z Finish!

What phrase did you find as you completed the maze?

_ _ _ _ _ _ _ _ _

Look at the crowns to the right, see if you can find the
one that's different in each row and color it purple!

Change one letter of the word to
see what words you can make:

P L A N

P L A

Brave to LIVE BOLDLY

KEY TRUTH
God is holy and perfect. Through Jesus, I can follow God and pattern my life after Him.

KEY VERSE
And one called to another: Holy, holy, holy is the LORD of Armies; his glory fills the whole earth.
Isaiah 6:3

KEY PASSAGE
The Holiness of God
(Isaiah 6)

The Holiness of God
BASED ON ISAIAH 6

In the year that King Uzziah died, Isaiah was worshiping God in the temple when he had a vision. Isaiah saw God sitting on a throne. God's robe was long; its edges filled the temple. Seraphim—heavenly beings—stood above Him, and they each had six wings. They called out: "Holy, holy, holy is the Lord; His glory fills the whole earth."

When the seraphim spoke, the foundations of the doorways shook, and the temple filled with smoke. Isaiah was in the presence of God!

He said, "I am ruined! I am sinful. I do not deserve to be in the presence of the King, the great and holy God."

Then one of the seraphim flew to Isaiah. The seraph had a burning coal from the altar in his hand. He touched Isaiah's mouth and said, "Now that this has touched your lips, your wickedness is removed and your sin is wiped away."

Then Isaiah heard God's voice: "Who should I send? Who will go for Us?"

Isaiah said, "Here am I! Send me."

"Go," God said.

God told Isaiah an important message for the people.

This was God's message: "You will listen, but you will not understand. You will look, but you will not really see. If your eyes and ears and minds worked, you would turn from your sin and be healed."

Isaiah asked, "How long should I preach to people who won't listen?"

God answered Isaiah, "Preach until the cities are destroyed and no one lives in them. I am going to send the people far away."

Then God explained that He would bring some of the people back to Judah.

These people were part of Abraham's family. God was going to keep His promise to Abraham through them. He would send the Messiah through their family to be a blessing to all the nations.

SET APART

Draw something that stood out to you from today's Bible story.

What surprised you most in this passage of Scripture?

_____

_____

How do you imagine you would have responded if you were Isaiah?

_____

How would you explain the word _holy_?

_____

WHAT IS WORSHIP?

Complete the definition for worship and fill in the boxes according to your leader's instructions.

Worship is _____ _____ _____ _____

and _____ _____ to _____.

DAY ONE
Dreams

In the daydream bubble on the left, write or draw what you imagine your life might be like when you are older. Do you want to have a job? A pet? Be married? Own a car? Have kids? Where do you want to live?

It is great to have dreams for your life. We may or may not get everything we dream of, and that's okay. But we can trust that when we pattern our lives after Jesus, we get something better than we could ever dream!

We can't know exactly what God's plans are for our lives, but we know God is holy and perfect. And if He is perfect, that means we can trust whatever He has for us. If we are going live boldly and confidently in who God is and who He made us to be, we'll want to pattern our lives after Jesus and follow what His Word says.

Open your Bible to Psalm 119:33. This verse is a prayer to God for Him to direct our steps according to His Word.

PRAY
In the space below, write a prayer to God asking Him to direct your steps and to help you love what He has planned for your life.

_____

_____

_____

_____

DAY TWO
Filled with Jesus

Write in the balloon what you would need to fill it up with to make it float. If we put water in a balloon, it may be great for a water balloon fight, but it won't float in the air. If we put sand in a balloon, it sinks to the ground and doesn't float. If we put air in a balloon, it can be filled, but it may not stay in the air. Helium is the gas we put in balloons to make them float.

Just like a balloon is made to float with the right substance inside of it, if we are to pattern our lives after Jesus, we need to fill our lives with certain things.

Open your Bible to Philippians 4:8 and fill in the blanks.

WHATEVER IS _____

WHATEVER IS _____

WHATEVER IS _____

WHATEVER IS _____

WHATEVER IS _____

WHATEVER IS _____

WHATEVER IS _____

WHATEVER IS _____

These are things we can fill our lives with as we live boldly. Circle one on the list that you need to work on. Put a star by one you are filling up with pretty well.

PRAY

Dear God, help us fill our lives with what is true, noble, right, pure, lovely, and admirable. Please help us get rid of lies and negative thoughts and fill up with things that help us pattern our lives after You. In Jesus' name, amen.

DAY THREE
Hide God's Word in Your Heart

Write out the title of your favorite song next to the music notes.

♪♫ _____

How many times a week do you sing your favorite song? (Circle one.)

1   2   3   4   5+

The reason you are so familiar with your favorite song is that you probably repeat it all the time. Sometimes we think it is hard to memorize Bible verses, but that is just because we might be unfamiliar with them. Think about it—you probably couldn't sing your favorite song from memory after the first time you heard it. It probably took you repeating the song over and over to know it by heart. The same is true with Scripture.

Read Psalm 119:11. As you look at the verse below, draw the following symbols above certain words:

I - draw a 😊 for yourself   SIN - draw an ✕
HEART - draw a 🖤   YOU - draw a ✝

I HAVE TREASURED YOUR WORD IN MY HEART SO THAT I MAY NOT SIN AGAINST YOU. PSALM 119:11 (CSB)

You may love your favorite song, but I doubt that song can change your life. Guess what—God's Word can. When we hide God's Word in our heart, it helps us obey and follow Him. Consider memorizing this Bible verse this week. Write your Scripture on a card and put it where you see it all the time. You can even make up a tune to help you memorize the verse you chose. Say it often, but as you hide it in your heart, ask God to help it change the way you live.

PRAY

Dear God, thank You for Your Word. Please help me hide it in my heart, but also help it change the way I live. I want to live boldly for You, so please help me make time to hide Your Word in my heart.

DAY FOUR
Bold to Obey

Unscramble the goal of each leader.

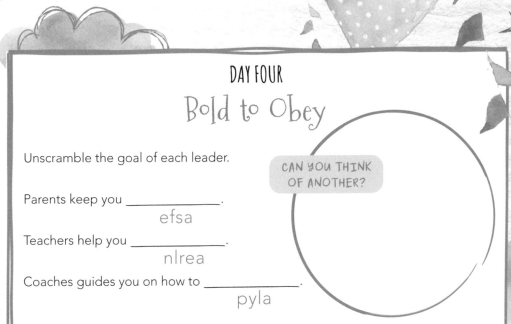

CAN YOU THINK
OF ANOTHER?

Parents keep you _____.
efsa

Teachers help you _____.
nlrea

Coaches guides you on how to _____.
pyla

Each of these leaders has a role to fill, but even more importantly, God does too. More than anyone, God knows what is best for you. That is why He longs for you to trust Him and obey Him.

Open your Bible to Psalm 112:1. In this verse we learn that people who are most happy and blessed are those who fear the Lord.

What do you think it means to fear the Lord?

_____

_____

Fearing God doesn't mean you are scared of Him. It means that you honor and respect God and are happy to obey Him because you believe that He knows what is best for you. God is holy and perfect. This is why we honor and respect Him. Through Jesus, we can follow God and pattern our lives after Him.

PRAY

Dear God, help me know what it means to fear, honor, and respect You. I believe that You know what is best for me. Help me be brave and bold to obey You. In Jesus' name, amen.

DAY FIVE
What Is Brave?

Write or draw what you think it looks like to be brave.

When in life can you start living bravely for God? (Circle your answer.)

NEVER   WHEN I AM OLDER   RIGHT NOW

Sometimes we think we have to be older or really physically strong to be brave. But bravery is more about what is on the inside than the outside.

Think about the young shepherd boy David, who agreed to fight the giant Goliath. He certainly didn't have the physical strength to take down a giant, but He knew God was on his side.

Look at 1 Samuel 17:47. There were two men on the field ready to fight, but whose battle does this verse say it is?

What is something you need to be brave for in your life right now?

Remember, God is holy and perfect. With God on your side, you have all you need to live boldly for Him!

PRAY

Dear God, I need Your help being brave. I can't do it on my own. Help me trust You when I am afraid. I need Your help being brave with the thing I just wrote about. Give me bravery to know that You are all I need. In Jesus' name, amen.

Journaling

Is there anything God is teaching you about Himself this week?
Have you learned anything about yourself?
Is there anything you want to spend time talking to God about?

Use these journal pages to write out your thoughts, questions, and prayers to God. Thank Him for teaching you about how to live as His brave girl and trusting in Him no matter what!

Things to Talk to God About

Games & Such

Draw what you would pack if your destination was unknown.

H 🌻
P ✕
R 🖤
S ☀
T 🩶
V ⭐
W 👑

_ _ _ at
i_ you_
fa_ _ o _ i_ e
_ ay _ o
_ _ o _ _ _ _ i _ ?

RIDDLES

Q: What travels around the world but stays in one corner?

A: A stamp!

Q: Where can you find an ocean without water?

A: A map!

Q: How do you know elephants love to travel?

A: They always pack their own trunks!

Brave to LOVE FIERCELY

KEY TRUTH

God loves and values all
people. He calls me to
live bravely and love like He loves.

KEY VERSE

Truly I tell you, wherever this gospel is proclaimed
in the whole world, what she has done will also be
told in memory of her.
Matthew 26:13 (CSB)

KEY PASSAGE

Jesus Was Anointed
(Matthew 26:6-13; Mark 14:3-9; John 12:1-8)

Jesus Was Anointed
BASED ON MATTHEW 26:6-13; MARK 14:3-9; JOHN 12:1-8

The time was coming to celebrate the Passover. Every year, the Jewish people gathered together to remember a special event that happened long ago. When God's people were slaves in Egypt, God did great things to rescue His people. The pharaoh saw God's power and authority, and the pharaoh let God's people go. God had used Moses to lead His people out of Egypt and to the promised land. God did not want the people to forget that time, so every year, the Jews had a feast. Many Jews traveled to Jerusalem to celebrate.

Six days before the Passover feast began, Jesus went to the town of Bethany. Bethany was near Jerusalem, and Jesus' friend Lazarus lived there with his sisters, Mary and Martha.

Jesus went to His friend Simon's house for a meal. Jesus was reclining at the table when Lazarus's sister Mary came to Him. She had a jar of very expensive oil. The oil smelled good, like a perfume. Mary broke open the jar and poured the oil on Jesus' head and feet.

Jesus' disciples were very upset! They thought Mary had wasted the expensive oil by pouring it on Jesus. The oil was worth 300 denarii—about a year's pay. One of the disciples, Judas Iscariot (iss KAR ih aht), said, "She could have sold the oil for a lot of money, and then she could have given the money to the poor!" Judas did not say this because he cared about the poor; he said it because he loved money. In fact, he was a thief.

They told Mary that she had done the wrong thing, but Jesus spoke up. "Leave her alone," He said. "She has done a very good thing for Me."

Then Jesus explained, "You will always have people around you who are poor, but you will not always have Me. Mary has poured oil on My body to get it ready for burial."

Jesus said that wherever the gospel was told in the whole world, people would also hear about Mary and what she had done.

VALUING ALL PEOPLE

God calls us to live bravely and love like He loves. Take a moment to reflect on the people God wants you to love. Your answers are for your eyes only.

Someone who is hard for me to love is _____

(You can write his or her initials.)

Someone I need to include more with my friends is _____

I have been guilty of gossiping about someone.

YES　　　　　NO　　　　　I'M NOT SURE

A friend I need to invite to church is _____

I have made fun of someone before.

YES　　　　　NO　　　　　I'M NOT SURE

Are there people I treat differently because they don't look like me?

YES　　　　　NO　　　　　I'M NOT SURE

I am a safe person who friends can confide in.

YES　　　　　NO　　　　　I WANT TO BE

A person's heart is more important to me than how she looks or dresses.

YES　　　　　NO　　　　　I'M NOT SURE

I look for people who need a friend.

YES　　　　　NO　　　　　I'M NOT SURE

I am brave and stand up for people when no one else will.

YES　　　　　NO　　　　　I WANT TO BE

I am brave and stand up for what I believe about Jesus.

YES　　　　　NO　　　　　I WANT TO BE

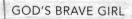

PASSAGE COMPARISON

List all of the differences and similarities you find in the passages listed below.

DIFFERENCES

MATTHEW 26:6-13	MARK 14:3-9	JOHN 12:1-8

SIMILARITIES

DAY ONE

R-E-S-P-E-C-T

Did you know that God loves and values all people? That girl that isn't nice to you—He loves and values her. That person who looks and dresses completely different than you—He loves and values her, too. Okay, get ready for some really big news. When it comes to boys—yep, you guessed it—God loves and values them, too. Genesis 1:27 helps us understand why God loves and values all people.

> **GOD CREATED MAN IN HIS OWN IMAGE; HE CREATED HIM IN THE IMAGE OF GOD; HE CREATED THEM MALE AND FEMALE. GENESIS 1:27 (CSB)**

Circle the part of the Scripture that says how God created us.

How does it make you feel to know you were created in the image of God? Draw a face in the circle that shows how you feel.

Nothing else God created was made in His image—not animals, not plants, not even angels. God created us like Him. He wants us to live bravely and love like He loves.

Who is someone that is hard to love that you can show God's love to?

_____

No matter how they act, what they wear, where they live, or what they have done wrong—God loves and values all people. If God loves and values them and we are made in His image, shouldn't we love them, too?

PRAY

Dear God, thank You for making all people in Your image. You set a great example by valuing all people. Help me remember that You made boys in your image, too, and I need to love them like You do. Because I am made in Your image, I can live bravely for You. In Jesus' name, amen.

DAY TWO
His Love Never Changes

Have you ever been separated from someone you love? Maybe you got lost and couldn't find your parents. Or maybe someone you care for very much moved far away.

How does it make you feel to be separated from someone you love?

SAD   HAPPY   AFRAID   I DON'T KNOW

Well, I have great news for you. Not only does God love and value all people—His love never changes. That's right, nothing can stop God's love. Nothing.

Open your Bible to Romans 8:38-39. Read through the verses carefully and list all the things that can't separate you from God's love.

_____ _____ _____ _____

_____ _____ _____ _____

How does it make you feel to know nothing can separate you from God?

SCARED   HAPPY   SAFE   CONFUSED

Because of this great love God has for us, we are called to love others like He does. Write the names of three people you know who need to hear that God loves them.

_____ _____ _____

PRAY

Dear God, what an amazing gift to know Your love is so perfect that nothing can separate us from it. You are more powerful than all the circumstances we may face, and we can count on Your love. God, the people I wrote above need to hear about Your love. Will You give me a chance to share it with them? In Jesus' name, amen.

DAY THREE
Speaking Truth in Love

Draw a picture of something embarrassing that has happened to you.

True friends sometimes have to tell each other hard and embarrassing stuff. Actually, one way of loving like God loves is to speak the truth in love. That means even if it may hurt someone's feelings a little bit, sometimes we have to say hard things to our friends or even hear hard things from our friends.

Has an adult or family member ever had to share something hard with you? Maybe she was correcting something you were doing wrong and it hurt a little at first, but you know it was for the best and said in love.

God's Word gives us good guidance on this topic. Read Proverbs 27:6 and match which action goes with which according to the verse.

WOUNDS OF A FRIEND   ARE EXCESSIVE

KISSES OF ENEMY   ARE TRUSTWORTHY

Now, this verse doesn't give us a free pass to say anything we want to other people. Remember, we are to love others like God loves. So He wouldn't say anything that wasn't true or necessary.

PRAY
Dear God, our words can be so powerful. Help my words be full of love so that I can build my friend up instead of tearing her down. Help me be a friend who speaks the truth in love. Even when it is hard, help me love others like You do. In Jesus' name, amen.

A Not-So-Funny Joke

If my mom told me once, she told me a million times, "Think before you speak." See, I thought just because I said something I thought was funny, it meant that it wouldn't hurt someone's feelings. It was supposed to be funny after all.

I had to learn the hard way with several friends that sometimes things we think are funny are very hurtful to people.

Has someone ever said something to you that she thought was funny but it hurt your feelings? (Circle your answer.)

YES   NO

Our words are very powerful. Read Proverbs 18:21 in your Bible. What two things are in the power of the tongue?

_____   _____

Have you ever used your words to hurt someone? (Circle your answer.)

YES   NO   If yes, who? _____

Have you told that person you are sorry? (Circle your answer.)

YES   NO

When we know that God loves and values all people, we learn that we are to love others like He does. We can start with our words.

PRAY

Dear God, I am sorry for the times I have hurt others with my words. Please make me aware that my words have power and help me use them carefully. Help me know the difference between being funny and being mean. In Jesus' name, amen.

DAY FIVE
Love to Love

List the things you have done to deserve God's love.

_____

While we may think we have done something to deserve God's love, we haven't. God's love is different from others'. No one deserves God's kind of love. God's love is a gift. Cross out your answer above and then write words that describe God's love in the gift box.

Since we didn't earn this amazing love, should we make others earn our love? Read John 13:34-35 in your Bible. Answer the following questions:

In what way are we to love others?

_____

How will people know we are His disciples?

_____

Who is someone you know who is hard to love? _____

List ways you can show her the love of God this week:

_____

PRAY

Dear God, help me see clearly that I did nothing to deserve Your love. Your love can't be earned, so I need to give it freely to everyone whether I think she deserves it or not. Help me show Your love to my person listed above. In Jesus' name, amen.

Journaling

Is there anything God is teaching you about Himself this week?
Have you learned anything about yourself?
Is there anything you want to spend time talking to God about?

Use these journal pages to write out your thoughts, questions, and prayers to God. Thank Him for teaching you about how to live as His brave girl, trusting in Him no matter what!

Things to Talk to God About

Games & Such

What are some ways you feel loved? Fill the jar with as many as you can think of.

Brave to PRAY FEARLESSLY

KEY TRUTH

Prayer is talking and listening to God. When I pray, I can praise Him, ask Him for help, and confess sin to Him. God wants me to pray to Him, confident that He hears and answers my prayers.

KEY VERSE

And Mary said: "My soul magnifies the Lord." Luke 1:46 (CSB)

KEY PASSAGE

Mary's Prayer (Luke 1:46-55)

Mary's Prayer
BASED ON LUKE 1:46-55

One day, God sent an angel named Gabriel to a town called Nazareth. The angel went to visit a young virgin named Mary. She was engaged to be married to Joseph, a descendant of King David.

The angel said to Mary, "Rejoice! You have found favor with God. He is with you." Mary was very afraid and puzzled. Why would God find favor with her? She had done nothing special.

"Do not be afraid," the angel said. Then he told Mary that she was going to have a very special and unique baby, and they would call the baby Jesus, which means "the Lord saves." The angel explained that the baby would be great—He would be God's Son! He would even be a King—the King God had promised would come.

Mary asked the angel, "How can that happen? I am not married yet." The angel replied, "God will be the Father of the baby. The baby will be God's Son."

Then the angel told Mary, "Nothing will be impossible with God!" He said that Mary's relative Elizabeth was pregnant even though she was old and did not have any children.

"May everything happen just as you said," Mary replied. Then the angel left her. Mary hurried to her relative Elizabeth's house. When she arrived, the baby inside Elizabeth leaped for joy! The Holy Spirit filled Elizabeth, and she said, "What an honor, Mary! Your baby will be blessed too!"

Mary was so happy. She praised God with a song about how great God is. Her song went like this:

My soul praises the greatness of the Lord, and my spirit rejoices in God my Savior, because He has looked with favor on the humble condition of His servant. Surely, from now on all generations will call me blessed, because the Mighty One has done great things for me, and His name is holy. His mercy is from generation to generation on those who fear Him. He has done a mighty deed with His arm; He has scattered the proud because of the thoughts of their hearts; He has toppled the mighty from their thrones and exalted the lowly. He has satisfied the hungry with good things and sent the rich away empty. He has helped His servant Israel, remembering His mercy to Abraham and His descendants forever, just as He spoke to our ancestors.

MARY'S PRAYER—LUKE 1:46-55 (CSB)

And Mary said:

My soul magnifies the Lord, and my spirit rejoices in God my Savior, because he has looked with favor on the humble condition of his servant. Surely, from now on all generations will call me blessed, because the Mighty One has done great things for me, and his name is holy. His mercy is from generation to generation on those who fear him. He has done a mighty deed with his arm; he has scattered the proud because of the thoughts of their hearts; he has toppled the mighty from their thrones and exalted the lowly. He has satisfied the hungry with good things and sent the rich away empty. He has helped his servant Israel, remembering his mercy to Abraham and his descendants forever, just as he spoke to our ancestors.

SONGS OF PRAISE

Write your own praise song like Mary's on the lines below. Color in the names of God on the next page and use them for inspiration!

_____

_____

_____

_____

_____

Alpha Omega
Lord of Lords
Counselor
Almighty
Savior
Lamb of
God
Prince of
Peace Abba
Redeemer Father
Emmanuel Jesus
Jehovah
Creator
Light of
the World
King of Kings
I AM
Messiah

How to Pray

List five things that happened today:

01. _____

02. _____

03. _____

04. _____

05. _____

Those things may seem big or small, but guess what—they all matter to God. Look back at your list above. Which of those things have you talked to God about today?

What are things that distract you or stop you from talking to God?

_____

_____

You may be nervous you won't say the right thing or that God is too busy to listen to you, but that isn't true. Prayer is talking and listening to God. God wants you to pray to Him, and He longs to hear about the big and little things of your day.

PRAY

Dear God, help me be confident in talking to You. You are listening even right now. I want to be brave to pray fearlessly, and I know You will help me. In Jesus' name, amen.

DAY TWO

Praise

What is something that excites you so much, you can't stop cheering for it?

_____

When we are excited about something, we can't stop cheering. We want to say all the good things about it we can.

That's the kind of energy and excitement we should have when praising God. When we praise God, we are honoring Him for who He is. Praising God also gets personal. Who has God been to you lately? (Circle the words that describe who God has been to you.)

FATHER   PEACE   PROTECTOR   COMFORT

FORGIVER   DEPENDABLE   CARING

SAVIOR   FRIEND   LOVING   AMAZING

CREATOR   HOPE   JOY   LORD

As you close in prayer, fill in the blanks with some of the words you circled.

PRAY

Dear God, You are _____, _____, and _____. There is no one like You. Thank You for being who You are and hearing my prayers. Help me always make time to talk to You. In Jesus' name, amen.

DAY THREE
Don't Be Afraid

Are there certain things that scare you? Look at the things on the list below. Place a *Y* by the things that scare you and an *N* by the things that don't scare you.

Is there anything else you can think of that might scare you that is not pictured?

There is plenty in this world we might be afraid of, but that doesn't mean we have to be.

Open your Bible to 2 Timothy 1:7. This verse helps us understand that fear is not from God. If we step back and take a long look at our fears, we can see that not all fears make sense.

God doesn't want us to be afraid. Fear can get in our way and stop us from doing things God has planned for us. Here is one thing that helps with fear: When your mind keeps thinking about what you are scared of, begin talking to God. Replace what is in your mind with a conversation with God. You can be confident that He hears your prayers.

PRAY

Dear God, please help me when I am afraid. Bring my mind back to Your truths so my fears don't stop me from doing what You have planned for my life. In Jesus' name, amen.

DAY FOUR
Pray for Others

Who is someone you know that you could pray for? Write his or her name below.

_____

While we can certainly talk to God about ourselves, God also wants us to pray for others, too.

Open your Bible to Ephesians 1:17-18. This is a great passage to pray for someone else:

I pray that the God of our Lord Jesus Christ, the glorious Father, would give **you** the Spirit of wisdom and revelation in the knowledge of him. I pray that the eyes of **your** heart may be enlightened so that **you** may know what is the hope of his calling, what is the wealth of his glorious inheritance in the saints.
—_Ephesians 1:17-18 (CSB)_

In the prayer below, rewrite the words in bold with the name of the person you know needs prayer.

I PRAY THAT THE GOD OF OUR LORD JESUS CHRIST, THE GLORIOUS FATHER, WOULD GIVE _____ THE SPIRIT OF WISDOM AND REVELATION IN THE KNOWLEDGE OF HIM. I PRAY THAT THE EYES OF _____ 'S HEART MAY BE ENLIGHTENED SO THAT _____ MAY KNOW WHAT IS THE HOPE OF HIS CALLING, WHAT IS THE WEALTH OF HIS GLORIOUS INHERITANCE IN THE SAINTS.

Not only can you pray for people you know, you can also pray for people around the world that you have never met, like **missionaries**, **people who need to hear about Jesus**, or **world leaders** who don't love Jesus. Which one of these will you commit to pray for this week? Underline it in the previous sentence.

PRAY

Dear God, what a gift it is to be able to talk to the Creator of the universe. Help me not only pray for myself but pray for others. Bring to my mind people who need prayer and help me set aside time to pray for them. In Jesus' name, amen.

DAY FIVE
Brush Daily

What is something you wish you could do all the time and it never stopped?

GO TO THE BEACH   PLAY OUTSIDE   PLAY WITH TOYS

Sometimes we wish things would never stop. Did you know there is a verse in the Bible about that? The Bible verse is just two words. Open your Bible to 1 Thessalonians 5:17 and complete the verse below.

Pray _____.

The more we spend time talking and listening to God, the more our relationship with Him grows. When we pray, we can praise Him, ask Him for help, and confess our sin to Him. God wants us to pray to Him, confident that He hears and answers our prayers.

Think of it like brushing your teeth. How many times a week is it best to brush your teeth? _____ What if you only brushed your teeth once or twice a week? Would your teeth be healthy? The more you brush your teeth, the healthier they are.

Think of this like praying. If you just talk to God once or twice a week, think about all you miss out on. God's Word tells us to pray constantly, so let's get started on that now.

PRAY

Dear God, we can never talk or listen to You too much. There are so many things to praise You for, so many things to confess to You, and so many people to pray for. Help me make prayer a priority, something I never want to end. In Jesus' name, amen.

Journaling

Is there anything God is teaching you about Himself this week?
Have you learned anything about yourself?
Is there anything you want to spend time talking to God about?

Use these journal pages to write out your thoughts, questions, and prayers to God. Thank Him for teaching you about how to live as His brave girl, trusting in Him no matter what!

_____

_____

_____

_____

_____

_____

_____

_____

_____

_____

_____

_____

_____

_____

_____

_____

_____

_____

_____

Things to Talk to God About

_____

_____

_____

_____

_____

_____

Games & Such

Circle all the items that help us communicate. *Hint: Some might not be used anymore!*

C O N V E R S A T I O N
P D I L T M G V U C V L
M O X Y B O N A T V H J
B C O N F E S S Z A O E
D M U T R M Q K U R L D
U N A H U D D A I L Y K
N P R A Y E R Q T T S S
H Q U N B I O Q A H P C
I R E K L B L P M A I I
V J N S G R A C E L R P
U O W R U Q S T N I I E
H F A R O K G U B Q T V

Find the following words in the word search:
CONFESS ASK THANKS PRAYER TALK AMEN
HOLY SPIRIT CONVERSATION GRACE DAILY

Brave to THRIVE WILLINGLY

KEY TRUTH

God calls me to continue becoming more like Jesus by the power of the Holy Spirit. I can thrive by growing deeper in my faith and living on mission for God.

KEY VERSE

Yet even now I know that whatever you ask from God, God will give you.
John 11:22 (CSB)

KEY PASSAGE

Martha on a Mission
(Luke 10:38-42; John 11:1-44)

Martha on a Mission
BASED ON LUKE 10:38-42; JOHN 11:1-44

While Jesus and His disciples were traveling, Jesus entered a village, and a woman named Martha welcomed Him into her home. She had a sister named Mary, who sat at the Lord's feet and was listening to what He said. But Martha was distracted by her many tasks, and she came up and asked, "Lord, don't you care that my sister has left me to serve alone? So tell her to give me a hand." The Lord answered her, "Martha, Martha, you are worried and upset about many things, but one thing is necessary. Mary has made the right choice, and it will not be taken away from her."

Now let's fast-forward to see how Martha responded when she and her sister Mary were grieving their brother's death.

After Mary and Martha's brother Lazarus had died, Jesus came to them. At this time Lazarus had been in the tomb for four days. Many of the Jews had come to Martha and Mary to comfort them about their brother.

As soon as Martha heard that Jesus was coming, she went to meet Him, but Mary remained seated in the house.

Then Martha said to Jesus, "Lord, if You had been here, my brother wouldn't have died. Yet even now I know that whatever You ask from God, God will give You."

"Your brother will rise again," Jesus told her.

Martha said to Him, "I know that he will rise again in the resurrection at the last day."

Jesus said to her, "I am the resurrection and the life. The one who believes in Me, even if he dies, will live. Everyone who lives and believes in Me will never die. Do you believe this?"

"Yes, Lord," she told Him, "I believe You are the Messiah, the Son of God, who comes into the world."

Jesus went and mourned His dear friend Lazarus' death and then raised him from the dead. Lazarus came out of the tomb bound hand and foot with linen strips and with his face wrapped in a cloth.

Jesus said to them, "Unwrap him and let him go."

FRUIT PLEASE

Use the words in the bank to fill in the missing words in the verses below.

VINE   FRUIT   MORE   REMAIN   BRANCH   PRODUCE   ME

"I am the true _____, and my Father is the gardener. Every

branch in me that does not produce _____ he removes,

and he prunes every branch that produces fruit so that it will produce

_____ fruit. You are already clean because of the word I

have spoken to you. _____ in me, and I in you. Just as a

_____ is unable to _____ fruit by itself unless it

remains on the vine, neither can you unless you remain in _____."

JOHN 15:1-4 (CSB)

THRIVING OR NOT THRIVING

Read each statement and decide if you think Martha was thriving or not. Color in the picture to show your answer.

	YES	NO
When Jesus came to visit, Martha was distracted by her many tasks.	🌼	🪣
Martha complained to Jesus and told Him to ask Mary to help her.	🌼	🪣
After her brother died, Martha heard Jesus was on His way. Instead of waiting on Him, she ran out to meet Him.	🌼	🪣
When Martha came to Jesus, even though her brother had been dead for four days, she said to Him, "Yet even now I know that whatever you ask from God, God will give you."	🌼	🪣
If I took an honest look at my life now, would I be thriving or not thriving?	🌼	🪣

List as many things as you can think of that are "thriving."

_____   _____

_____   _____

_____   _____

_____   _____

_____   _____

_____   _____

_____   _____

_____   _____

_____   _____

DAY ONE
The Greatest Award

If you could receive any award, what would you want it to be? Write and decorate what that award would be on the ribbon.

You may have won many awards or very few, but what matters is how hard you work toward that goal. Giving your all is very important. Awards and being noticed are nice and all, but there is a greater award for us to work toward.

> WHATEVER YOU DO, DO IT FROM THE HEART, AS SOMETHING DONE FOR THE LORD AND NOT FOR PEOPLE, KNOWING THAT YOU WILL RECEIVE THE REWARD OF AN INHERITANCE FROM THE LORD. YOU SERVE THE LORD CHRIST.
> COLOSSIANS 3:23–24 (CSB)

Remember, whether you are on the ball field, in school, or at home, God wants you to know Him more and love others like He does. Knowing God is the greatest reward.

PRAY

Dear God, as nice as it is to get noticed or get awards, help me remember that what matters most is the goal of living for You. Teach me how to do everything with a heart that loves You most and loves other people like You do. In Jesus' name, amen.

Sharing About Jesus

Have you ever seen someone in need of something that you had and could share with them? Maybe your friend needed to borrow your eraser in the middle of a big test. Or maybe your younger sibling needed help with something around the house.

What are some items you like to share with others? Draw a picture of them.

Sharing seems simple sometimes, but other times it might be more difficult. Sometimes we see people in need of God's love and forgiveness, but we don't always share with them the good news of how they can know God.

If you have a relationship with Jesus, you are holding an incredible and powerful gift—the love of God. And you get to share that good news with others! God wants us to be brave to share His love with those who need to know Him. Don't worry, God is always with you when you tell others about Him! He calls us to continue becoming more like Jesus by the power of the Holy Spirit. The Holy Spirit helps us to be brave and tell others the great things God is teaching us about Himself. We can thrive by growing deeper in our faith and living on mission for God.

Who are some people you know that don't believe in God? Write their names in the blanks below.

_____

PRAY

Dear God, by the power of Your Holy Spirit, help me share Your love with the people I just listed. I want to live on mission for You, but I need Your help. As I spend more time with You, help me thrive so people see Jesus in me. In Jesus' name, amen.

DAY THREE

Jesus Changes Everything

Sometimes the Old Testament can be difficult to read. There are people fighting, God punishing nations, and all those animal sacrifices. Aren't you glad we don't have to do those sacrifices today? Well, what changed between the Old and New Testament? Look for the word hidden in the picture below. Color in the letters you see.

When Jesus came, He changed everything. There was no need for sacrifices because He was the once-for-all sacrifice who took the punishment we deserve for our sin—death. That is amazing news. Because of Jesus, we don't have to keep all the Old Testament commands perfectly. (We couldn't if we tried!) And we don't have to sacrifice animals. We don't have to do things to earn God's love or forgiveness. Instead, God wants us to receive the gift of salvation that Jesus gives.

HE SAVED US—NOT BY WORKS OF RIGHTEOUSNESS THAT WE HAD DONE, BUT ACCORDING TO HIS MERCY—THROUGH THE WASHING OF REGENERATION AND RENEWAL BY THE HOLY SPIRIT. TITUS 3:5 (CSB)

This Scripture proves that Jesus came to save us. He gave us mercy, which means He didn't give us what we deserve—death. Jesus changes everything.

PRAY

Dear God, thank You for Jesus. Thank You for giving us Your one and only Son to take our punishment for our sin. Help me see that I did nothing to deserve Your love. You give it freely, and I am so thankful. In Jesus' name, amen.

DAY FOUR
Growing Up in God

Do you know what you were like as a baby? Draw what you think you looked like during each stage of life.

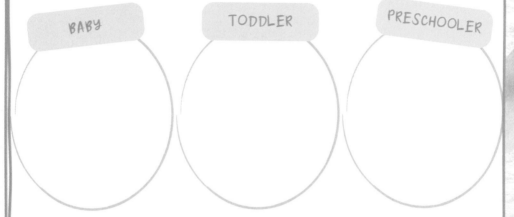

BABY TODDLER PRESCHOOLER

It is crazy to think we all started out as babies. There were so many things you didn't understand when you were a baby, but as you grew older you learned more and became wiser.

This is what it is like to follow God. When we begin we are like babies. We begin with very little knowledge of who He is, but as He teaches us, we grow to look more like Jesus. We don't do this on our own. God gives us a gift to help us.

Read John 14:26 in your Bible. Who is it that helps us grow to be more like Jesus?

Reading your Bible, studying God's Word, and spending time in prayer are all ways we can grow deeper in our faith. Then as we grow, we will thrive and be on mission for God.

PRAY
Dear God, thank You for teaching me about what it means to grow. Help me grow stronger and healthier. Thank You for sending Jesus. Please help me continue to grow to look more like Jesus. In Jesus' name, amen.

DAY FIVE
Follow the Leader

Circle any of the words below that you think describe Jesus.

SAVIOR   SON OF GOD   MEAN   SAFE   HONEST

UNLOVING   TRUSTWORTHY   ENVIOUS   SERVANT

GOOD   RECKLESS   ALL-KNOWING   HOLY

Did you circle the word "servant"? Jesus was unique in that He wasn't just our Savior; He was also a servant. Jesus, the Son of God, set the example for us on service.

Oftentimes we think we have to do big things to honor God. We think we need to be on stage, have lots of followers, or be in charge of something. But the Bible tells us what it takes to be great.

IT MUST NOT BE LIKE THAT AMONG YOU. ON THE CONTRARY, WHOEVER WANTS TO BECOME GREAT AMONG YOU MUST BE YOUR SERVANT. MATTHEW 20:26 (CSB)

That is the opposite of our thinking, isn't it? The Bible tells us that we are called to be more like Jesus by serving others. That means you, too! Just because you are younger doesn't mean you can't serve God.

If you want to live on mission for God, don't look for jobs so people can see you. Look for ways to serve God and point others to Him.

What are some ways you can serve God?

_____

_____

PRAY

Dear God, thank You that You gave us Jesus as the example of the greatest servant. Jesus is not only our Savior, He also set the example for what service should look like. Help me follow His example. In Jesus' name, amen.

Journaling

Is there anything God is teaching you about Himself this week?
Have you learned anything about yourself?
Is there anything you want to spend time talking to God about?

Use these journal pages to write out your thoughts, questions, and prayers to God. Thank Him for teaching you about how to live as His brave girl, trusting in Him no matter what!

Things to Talk to God About

_____   _____

_____   _____

_____   _____

_____   _____

_____   _____

_____   _____

Games & Such

Use the clues below to find out who is described. Fill the answers in the crossword to see if you're right!

What sorts of flowers or plants do you love? Draw a thriving potted plant below, and don't forget to decorate the pot!

DOWN

1 I was in a tomb for four days. Jesus called me out, and I was made alive again!

5 I tell people about a certain subject. Sometimes I give quizzes and ask questions.

ACROSS

2 I told Jesus I believed He was the Messiah. I also tried to get Jesus to make my sister help me.

3 I have a team that I lead. I help each person get better at playing the game.

4 Mary sat at My feet to listen. I wept for My friend's death and then raised him from the tomb.

6 I'm the younger of two sisters. Jesus said that I had made the right choice.

Reflections

TAKE A LOOK AT WHAT YOU'VE LEARNED!

HELLO MY NAME IS:

God has taught me…

_____

_____

_____

_____

_____

_____

Draw a picture of your favorite memory or something fun that happened from this study.

Being God's brave girl means…

_____

_____

_____

This week, I can live as God's brave girl by…

_____

_____

_____

I AM
God's
Brave
Girl

God is
ALWAYS
trustworthy

Pattern
YOUR LIFE
after
JESUS

i can
love
fiercely

GOD
ANSWERS
OUR
PRAYERS

I CAN GROW
DEEPER IN
MY FAITH

If you keep silent at this time, relief and deliverance will come to the Jewish people from another place, but you and your father's family will be destroyed. Who knows, perhaps you have come to your royal position for such a time as this.

ESTHER 4:14 (CSB)

I have come so that they may have life and have it in abundance.

JOHN 10:10 (CSB)

Truly I tell you, wherever this gospel is proclaimed in the whole world, what she has done will also be told in memory of her.

MATTHEW 26:13 (CSB)

And one called to another: Holy, holy, holy is the LORD of Armies; his glory fills the whole earth.

ISAIAH 6:3 (CSB)

Yet even now I know that whatever you ask from God, God will give you.

JOHN 11:22 (CSB)

And Mary said: "My soul magnifies the Lord."

LUKE 1:46 (CSB)